CW01052160

The Beginning of Everything

A study in GENESIS 1-11

Written for The Word Worldwide
'Geared for Growth' series
by Marie Dinnen

Preface

Welcome to this Word Worldwide 'Geared for Growth' Bible Study. It will encourage, challenge and enrich you as you follow it through. Its format makes it very suitable for group Bible study.

This study is made up of an Introduction and 10 Bible studies on Genesis 1-11. Easy-to-read Bible passages indicated for each day are followed by questions to help stimulate a greater understanding of the Bible and encourage positive sharing.

It is strongly recommended that when used in groups, group members should first read the set daily Bible passages at home and answer the questions (writing the answers down will help in learning). During the group meeting these Bible passages should then be reread and answers to the questions shared. The appropriate page of Notes should be read at the end of the study period together.

An Answer Guide is included at the end of this booklet.

Contact your nearest address on page 44 if who would like help to set up and run a Bible study group. A *Guidelines for Group Leaders* leaflet is also available from the same address.

> *'Exposing as many people as possible to the truths of God's Word, using Geared for Growth Bible Studies as a tool for evangelism, spiritual growth and the imparting of missionary vision.'*

Unless otherwise stated, quotations from the Bible are from the New International Version, © 1973, 1978, 1984 by International Bible Society, published in Great Britain by Hodder and Stoughton Ltd.

National Library of Australia Card Number and ISBN 0 908067 28 3
© WEC International

THE BEGINNING OF EVERYTHING

> The book of Genesis, seed plot of all
> Relates creation's story, and the fall,
> The flood, the call of Abraham and his seed,
> Their sojourn down in Egypt, and their need.

In this study we will look at the events recorded in Genesis 1-11. The remaining 39 chapters are covered in three other studies – the life of Abraham, of Jacob and of Joseph.

Genesis means origin or beginning. We are going to find out about the beginning of: the world – 1:1-25; the human race – 1:26-2:25; sin in the world – 3:1-7; God's plan of redemption– 3:8-24; family life – 4:1-15; man-made civilisation – 4:16–9:29; the nations of the world – 10:1-11:32; the Hebrew race – 12:1-2 (and onwards).

Genesis, because it tells of man's failure, could be a very discouraging study. However, it contains the promise of One who will: atone for man's sin – Romans 5:20-21; destroy the devil's power – 1 John 3:8; create everything new – Revelation 21:1-5; establish His everlasting Kingdom – Revelation 12:10; ... so it is an unfolding story of a Great Creator.

God does love those whom He has created and makes every provision for us to live at peace and in fellowship with Him.

Has a child ever asked you, 'Who made God?' I wonder what answer you gave!

Our human minds cannot understand that: God always was; eternity has no beginning or end; space knows no boundaries; the world was made from nothing.

The very mystery and wonder of all this makes us realise that there is a mind, personality, intelligence beyond our comprehension. We exhaust ourselves debating, arguing, researching, reasoning, deducing, and ultimately are forced to recognise the fact that there is a power beyond ourselves – a God in whom we can put our faith.

When we go to the Bible, God's Word to man, we may not initially fully comprehend its truths, but if we take a leap of faith and put our trust in what the Bible tells us, the Holy Spirit of God will give us spiritual understanding (John 16:13-14).

WHO WROTE THIS BOOK OF BEGINNINGS?
Bible scholars assess Moses to be the writer and their opinion is underlined by Scripture. Look up and discuss Matthew 19:8; Mark 12:26; Luke 16:31; John 1:45;John 5:46-47 (especially good in the Living Bible).

Since the 'Book of Moses' relates man's history from 2000 years before Moses was born, and Abraham, who lived 600 years before Moses, we can see how God wonderfully has preserved this record for all mankind. Much would have been handed down from generation to generation by word of mouth, but Moses had access to eleven sets of family records which covered creation's story and the history of Adam, Seth, Noah and his sons, Shem, Terah, Ishmael, Isaac, Esau and Jacob. God obviously gave Moses direct revelation, too, so what came from Moses' pen was God's Word. (See how he communicated God's instructions to the Israelites in Exodus 19:1-7.)

THE GENESIS STORY AND SCIENCE!

It would be so very easy to become involved in controversial discussion during these studies. Don't fall into the trap! More and more today science is agreeing with Scripture, we are told. To debate irreconcilable points is futile. Desire the spiritual revelation of truth that God wants to give us – this is life-giving. Scripture makes this point clear – see Deuteronomy 29:29.

OUR CREATOR

God's works are wonderful! Yet the One who is all-wonderful, our great Father-Creator-God, is the One who should be exalted as we pursue these studies. Let us encourage each other to know and love Him with all our hearts. Paul, in his letter to the Colossian Christians urges them (and us!) to put the emphasis where it belongs. Turn to Colossians 1:12-20. See what God has done for us, through Christ:

    v.12 He has made us sharers in His Kingdom
    v.13 He has rescued us from Satan's Kingdom
    v.14 He has bought our freedom with Christ's blood which cleanses from
            sin
    v.15 He has revealed Himself to us, in Christ
    v.16 He reminds us that He is the Creator of everything
    v.17 He holds everything together by His power
    v.18 He is the Head of His church
    v.19 He put all of Himself in His Son
    v.20 He has made peace with us through the blood of Christ.

May the wonder of all this be an increasing reality in our lives.

THE POWER OF GOD'S WORD

DAY 1   *Genesis 1:1-5; Proverbs 8:22; John 1:1.*
a) Who was present at the beginning of creation?
b) Who was the author of creation?
b) Write down simply what happened in Genesis 1:1-5 and discuss it.

DAY 2   *Genesis 1:6-8.*
a) What did God make next (Psalm 104:2; Proverbs 8:27)?
b) What was the result (Psalm 104:13; Proverbs 8:28)?

DAY 3   *Genesis 1:9-13.*
a) Now what did God do (Psalm 104:7-9; Proverbs 8:25)?
b) What next 'kingdom' did God create (Psalm 104:13-18)?

DAY 4   *Genesis 1:14-19; Psalm 104:19; Job 38:7,31-33.*
a) On this fourth day of creation what happened?
b) How did God accomplish these mighty acts (v.11; Psalm 33:9)?

DAY 5   *Genesis 1:20-23; Psalm 104:25.*
a) God spoke again. What happened?
b) What power was given to these creatures?

DAY 6   *Genesis 1:24-31.*
a) God now creates another kingdom. Which one?
b) What was special about the last creature God created?

DAY 7   *Genesis 2:1-3.*
a) What do these verses emphasise about creation?
b) Look up the following verses and see how they confirm this account of creation in Genesis: Nehemiah 9:6; Isaiah 40:28; 45:12; Hebrews 11:3.

THE POWER OF GOD'S WORD

Timelessness ...

Darkness ...

Nothingness ...

Silence ...

TIME TO BEGIN
'In the beginning God created the heavens and the earth' (Genesis 1:1).
'Through him all things were made; without him nothing was made that has been made' (John 1:3).
'The Spirit of God was hovering over the waters' (Genesis 1:2).

TIME TO SPEAK
God spoke. And His energising word produced light (v.3), separated the upper vapours from the lower water mass (v.6), caused dry land to emerge from the midst of the seas (v.9), created vegetation – grass, herb and tree – (v.11), placed the stars, the sun and the moon in space (vv.14-16), caused the waters to teem with aquatic life (v. 20), brought the animal kingdom into being (v.24). Finally, He made man in His own image (v.27).

God spoke in blessing to His created beings and said, 'Be fruitful and increase in number; fill the earth and subdue it' (v.28).

TIME TO REST
God was satisfied with His work. At each stage of development He declared that what He had done was good (vv.4,10,12,18, 21, 25) and finally, very good (v.31).

On the seventh day He rested. He ceased from His creative acts. But Christ declared in John 5:17, 'My Father is always at his work ... and I, too, am working'. God had plans beyond the stage of creation! We will find out how important that is to us.

'(God) rested on the seventh day. Therefore the LORD blessed the Sabbath day and made it holy' (Exodus 20:11).

TIME FOR US TO BEGIN!
Let the Bible speak to us.
'Faith cometh by hearing, and hearing by the word of God' (Romans 10:17, AV).

'All Scripture is God-breathed and is useful ... (2 Timothy 3:16).

'For prophecy never had its origin in the will of man, but men spoke from God as they were carried along by the Holy Spirit' (2 Peter 1:21).

'By faith we understand that the universe was formed at God's command, so that what is seen was not made out of things which are visible" (Hebrews 11:3).

TIME FOR US TO HEAR!
'In these last days he (God) has spoken to us by his Son' (Hebrews 1:2).

TIME FOR US TO SEE!
'For God who said , "Let light shine out of darkness," made his light shine in our hearts to give us the light of the knowledge of the glory of God in the face of Christ' (2 Corinthians 4:6).

Jesus Christ is the living 'Word' of God (John 1:1,14), the 'Light' of the world (John 8:12): 'in him is no darkness at all' (1 John 1:5).

TIME FOR US TO BELIEVE!
Faith can take the plunge, fully relying on God's Word, even when it does not understand. Scientists are increasingly acknowledging the God of Creation. What human mind can grasp the fact that God is One, yet more than One (Genesis 1:26)? Or, 'For a thousand years in your sight are like a day that has just gone by, or like a watch in the night' (Psalm 90:4)? Or, 'With the Lord a day is like a thousand years, and a thousand years are like a day' (2 Peter 3:8)?

TIME FOR US TO REST!
'"And on the seventh day God rested from all his work" ... There remains, then, a Sabbath-rest for the people of God' (Hebrews 4:4,9).

'Come to me, all you who are weary and burdened, and I will give you rest' (Matthew 11:28).

As we continue with these studies we should all be able to say with unshakeable conviction:

'I believe in God, the Father Almighty, Maker of heaven and earth ... and in Jesus Christ, His Son ...'

THE GARDEN OF GOD

DAY 1   *Genesis 2:4-7.*
a) What name is now given to God?
b) What verses in Genesis 1 correspond with Genesis 2:5?

DAY 2   *Genesis 2:7; 1 Corinthians 15:45,47.*
a) How did God make man?
b) How did He impart life to him?
c) Had He given life to His other creatures in a similar way?

DAY 3   *Genesis 2:8-14.*
a) Where did God plant a garden?
b) How would you describe this garden?
c) What two trees are specially mentioned?

DAY 4   *Genesis 2:15-17.*
a) What did the man have to do in the Garden of Eden?
b) How would the presence of the tree of the knowledge of good and evil be a test of man's loyalty and obedience to God?

DAY 5   *Genesis 2:16-17.*
a) If the man disobeyed God's instructions what would happen?
b) Deuteronomy 30:15-20; Psalm 1:1-2. What do these references say about the way to blessing?

DAY 6   *Genesis 2:18.*
a) What had God said after every act of creation (Genesis 1)?
b) How does Genesis 2:18 differ from this? What did God decide to do?

DAY 7   *Genesis 2:18-25, 1 Corinthians 11:9.*
a) Did the man find a companion amongst the animals?
b) How was the first woman Eve formed?
c) From what we have already read in Genesis, why did God institute marriage (Genesis 1:28; 2:18)?

THE GARDEN OF GOD

THE VALUE OF A SOUL
Dr. Henry Morris in the *Genesis Record* says, 'Rocks seem, to all appearances, to be composed of totally different substances than human flesh, but nevertheless modern science verifies that the two are made from basic chemical elements: nitrogen, oxygen, calcium. etc.' Even with inflation, the actual worth of a body is very little indeed!

What makes this clay frame so valuable?
The Life of God that was breathed into Adam's soul!

'None of the other creatures had the breath of God in them? Man was uniquely made in the likeness of God, and his soul, higher than those of the animal kingdom, required God's direct energizing for its activation' (Dr. Morris).

THE PARADISE OF GOD
Beginning with the flood, the geographical details recorded in Scripture have changed down the centuries. The Pishon and Gihon rivers have disappeared. The Tigris and Euphrates have no doubt changed their courses and their sources are now separated by a mountain range. It is still estimated that Eden was situated in South West Asia somewhere in the region of present day Iraq. Wherever it was, it was a paradise. Here God provided for man's needs - physical, mental, emotional and spiritual. The first man, at this stage, had no reason to ask, 'Why did you make me like this?' (Romans 9:20).

God placed everything under man's dominion (Genesis 1:28) and then God gave him the privilege and responsibility of caring for His garden.

In the middle of the garden was the 'tree of life' which, according to Genesis 3:22 bore fruit which would ensure that the eater would live forever. Revelation 22:2 speaks of this tree growing in the New Jerusalem for the 'healing' of the nations. Also in the middle of the garden was the 'tree of the knowledge of good and evil' whose fruit God forbade them to eat (Genesis 2:17). Since God had made everything 'good' it is unlikely that the fruit would be harmful. The issue must therefore be that 'death' would result from disobedience to God's instructions rather than from the effect of eating the fruit.

PARADISE COMPLETE
Nowhere in God's creation was there a partner for the man God had made. Yet God had told him to be fruitful, multiply and replenish the earth.

God caused Adam (which means man) whom He had made from dust (adamah) to fall into a deep sleep. He removed a rib from Adam's side and created from it a woman. 'The woman came into being from the very life of man. Life begets life' (Dr. Ronald Youngblood).

God Himself ordained marriage - one man with one woman becoming one flesh. And it is recorded for us today in Matthew 19:4-6 that no one should separate those whom He has made one.

As we study Scripture we find that marriage is an earthly counterpart of the relationship between Christ and His church – the Bride of Christ (Ephesians 5:25-32; Revelation 19:7; Revelation 21:2,9).

ENTER – THE ENEMY!

DAY 1   *Genesis 3:1-6; 23-24.*

a) Reflect on Genesis 1 and 2. What impression are you left with of God and His creation?

b) What new creature are we introduced to Genesis 3? What happens at the end of the chapter?

DAY 2   *Revelation 12:9; 20:1-3.*

a) By what other names is the serpent identified here?

b) What other titles are given to him in John 14:30; 2 Corinthians 4:4; Ephesians 2:2?

DAY 3   *Ezekiel 28:11-19.*

In this reference to the king of Tyre many see a description of Satan and his fall. What can we find out about him from this passage?

DAY 4   *Isaiah 14:12-15.*

This passage is similar to yesterday's reading.

a) What titles are given to Satan?

b) How does this passage add to our knowledge about Satan?

DAY 5   *Hebrews 1:14; Revelation 5:11-12; 21:9.*

What insights do these references give into what God's angels do?

DAY 6   *Matthew 13:19; John 8:44; 2 Corinthians 11:3.*

a) What glimpses do we get of Satan's character here?

b) Contrast this with what Satan should have been doing (DAY 5).

DAY 7   *Genesis 1:24-25,31.*

a) What did God say about the animal life He had created?

b) Genesis 3:1-5. How could something God created begin to lead the woman astray?

ENTER – THE ENEMY!

The Serpent is alive today, and comes to tempt us too! So let us try and share Eve's feelings in this momentous interview.

SATAN'S CONSPIRACY

Serpent: 'Really? None of the fruit in the garden? God says you mustn't eat any of it? Do you think He really loves you? Is it fair?"

Eve: 'Of course we may eat it. It's only the fruit from the tree at the centre of the garden that we are not to eat."

Serpent: (Looks at Eve pityingly, sympathising. Mutters under his breath) 'If I can only get her eyes off her beautiful Adam and on to that miserable fruit, I'll win.'

Eve: 'God says we mustn't eat it – or even touch it – we might die if we do.'

Serpent: 'What nonsense! Die if you touch it? Whoever heard of such a thing? You won't die if you touch it. Reach up now and grasp some of it!'

Eve: 'How beautiful it is!'

Serpent: (Under his breath) 'If I can get Adam's eyes off his Creator and on to the wretched fruit, I'll win!'

Adam: 'Is it good to eat?'

Serpent: 'Yes, it's good to eat. It's not poison. You won't die!'

Adam: 'Will it really give me wisdom?'

Serpent: (Under his breath) 'Of course, they are just like God already! But they have forgotten that. I must tell them to try and become like God.'
(Aloud) 'Certainly it will make you wise. In fact that's why God doesn't want you to eat it – why, you'd become like gods, you two – you'd know what's good and what's bad for you. You'd be equal to Him.'

Eve: 'I really feel I'd like some.'

Serpent: (Under his breath) 'As long as they are tied to His apron strings, and He
            decides everything for them, they don't need to know one thing about good
            or evil.'
            (Aloud) 'You've never known this before – but this lovely fruit will open
            your eyes!'

Adam: 'Won't we die?'

Serpent: (Under his breath) 'Now if I can get them to make their own choices,
            independent-like, regardless of God – why, I've got them!'
            (Aloud) 'Of course not! It's just what you both need. It will liberate you!'

            ... so they take it.

                        (Dialogue by Dr. Stuart Harverson)

Satan, given beauty and power by God, designed to be a servant of man, made in the
image of God, was not content with his position. It is absurd to think that one of God's
created beings could ever hope to be equal with Him, but Satan dared to compete with the
Eternal 'I am' (Exodus 3:14).

Dr. Henry Morris says:
'It may be possible that one of the factors that generated Satan's resentment against God
was God's plan for mankind, i.e. to be uniquely "in the image-likeness of God". They
were also to reproduce their own kind, neither of which blessings was shared by Lucifer
or the angels. This may be the reason why God cast Satan to earth and not directly to the
lake of fire – to enable him to tempt man to fall as he himself had fallen. Perhaps the devil
believed that, by capturing man's dominion and affection, along with the allegiance of
his own fallen angels, he might even yet be able to ascend to heaven and dethrone God.'

Scripture leaves such detail obscure. However, we are left in no doubt as to Satan's
character and power. Do not be dismayed! Memorise this verse: 'The reason the Son of
God appeared was to destroy the devil's work' (1 John 3:8).

PARADISE SPOILED!

DAY 1   *Genesis 3:1-2.*
a) What was the devil's first approach to Eve? How accurate was her reply (Genesis 2:17)?
b) Discuss the dangers of tampering with God's Word (Deuteronomy 4:2; Revelation 22:18-19).

DAY 2   *Genesis 3:4-6.*
a) What further tactics did the devil employ?
b) Was the woman deceived? What about Adam (Romans 5:12)?

DAY 3   *Genesis 3:6.*
a) On what three levels was Eve tempted (1 John 2:16)?
b) How could she (or we!) have withstood temptation (Ephesians 6:13-18)?

DAY 4   *Genesis 3:5-10,22.*
a) Which part of Satan's prediction (v.5) came true?
b) What immediate effects of sin are evident?

DAY 5   *Genesis 3:11-14,16-19,22-24.*
a) How did Adam and Eve both respond to God's questions?
b) What effects of sin are highlighted by God's judgment pronounced on Adam and Eve?

DAY 6   *Genesis 3:15.*
a) How many sets of antagonists do we see here?
b) How would a crushing blow against the devil be achieved (Matthew 1:20-21; Hebrews 2:14; 1 John 3:8)?

DAY 7   *Genesis 3:21.*
a) God's judgment was tempered with mercy. How did He deal with Adam and Eve's nakedness and shame?
b) By reading John 1:29,36; Hebrews 9:22, how can we see that what God did for Adam and Eve foreshadowed something to come?

PARADISE SPOILED

TEMPTATION
Temptation comes from the devil and always seeks to force us to contravene God's laws. James 1:14-15 says: 'Each one is tempted when, by his own evil desire, he is dragged away and enticed. Then, after desire has conceived, it gives birth to sin; and sin, when it is full-grown, gives birth to death.'

TESTING
Testing comes from God and is always to increase our faith in Him and make us spiritually strong. James 1:12 says, 'Blessed is the man who perseveres under trial, because when he has stood the test, he will receive the crown of life that God has promised to those who love Him.'

JESUS
Jesus was under both test and temptation at the beginning of His public ministry. 'Jesus ... led by the Spirit in the desert, ... was tempted by the devil' (Luke 4:1-2).
He never faltered, but remained true to God and fought the devil with the Word of God: 'It is written (says) ...' (see Luke 4:4,8,12).

BODILY APPETITES
We saw how Eve was tempted on three levels. Satan will come to us in similar ways. The temptations of Jesus in the wilderness followed the same pattern:
Appeal to the physical appetite (Luke 4:3-4).
Appeal to emotional desires (Luke 4:5-8)
Appeal to spiritual pride (Luke 4:9-12).
He was tempted on every point, just as we are, yet did not sin (Hebrews 4:15) and is therefore to sustain us if we turn to Him when we are tempted (Hebrews 2:18).

THE CURSE
The blight of God's judgment and spiritual death were ushered in when Adam sinned. Adam was created to rule the earth. Now he was helpless to save himself and his dominion from destruction. Romans 8:22 says that: 'the whole creation has been groaning as in the pains of childbirth right up to the present time.'

Yet God left Adam and Eve with a promise that sin and death would be remedied (Genesis 3:15) and in Romans we read, 'For the whole creation was subjected to frustration, not by its own choice, but by the will of the one who subjected it, in hope that the creation itself will be liberated from its bondage to decay and brought into the glorious freedom of the children of God' (Romans 8:19-21).

The Seed of the woman came. 'Christ redeemed us from the curse of the law by becoming a curse for us, ... that we might receive the promise of the Spirit' (Galatians 3:13-14).

God has His plans well in hand. Compare the sad picture of Genesis with the bright future of Revelation. Here are just a few of the changes ahead for those who love God.

Genesis	Revelation
Sun, moon (1:16)	No need of sun or moon (21:23)
God walking in the garden (3:8)	God dwelling with His people (21:3)
Curse (3:17)	No more curse (22:3)
Daily sorrow (3:17)	No more sorrow (21:4)
Returning to dust (3:19)	No more death (21:4)
Continual evil (6:5)	Nothing that defiles (21:27)
Satan opposing (3:15)	Satan banished (20:10)
Redeemer promised (3:15)	Redemption accomplished (5:9-10)

LOST MEN IN A LOST WORLD

DAY 1   *Genesis 3:21; 4:1-5; Hebrews 11:4.*
a) What were the names and occupations of Adam and Eve's two sons?
b) Can you think why God looked with favour on Abel and his offering?

DAY 2   *Genesis 4:6-12.*
a) How far did Cain's jealousy and anger push him?
b) How was this further 'curse' going to affect Cain?

DAY 3   *Genesis 4:13-17.*
a) Though pronouncing judgment on Cain, did God abandon him? What did He do?
b) How did Cain go about making a new life for himself?

DAY 4   *Genesis 4:18-24; 2:23-24.*
a) Which generation after Adam defied God's marriage principle?
b) Who committed the second recorded murder?

DAY 5   *Genesis 4:25-5:2; 1:27.*
a) What happened after Seth was born?
b) What was the first important fact Adam recorded in his family history?

DAY 6   *Genesis 5:3-20.*
a) What part of God's curse on Adam comes to pass here (Genesis 3:19)?
b) Look at the genealogy and ages recorded. This is your family history!

DAY 7   *Genesis 5:21-32.*
a) What two important things are said here about Enoch?
b) How long did Methuselah live?
c) What do you discover about Methuselah's grandson in verses 28-32?

LOST MEN IN A LOST WORLD

CONFLICT

As God predicted (Genesis 3:15) the offspring of the serpent and of the women would be at enmity. Adam and Eve had been made aware that innocent blood had to be shed to atone for sin and enable them to draw near to God (Genesis 3:21). Whether animal sacrifice was instituted at this point or not is obscure, but Cain and Abel would have been well aware of the principle. Abel's offering of a blood sacrifice indicated a heart acknowledging its guilt, and bowing to God's will. Cain's offering, produced by his own effort, indicated a proud, unyielding heart. Look up and discuss Ephesians 2:8-9. The two brothers typified opposing forces – the one 'for' and the other 'against' God.

The same situation held in Christ's day when the religious leaders (described by Christ as belonging 'to your father, the devil' – John 8:44) chose to shed His innocent blood rather than obey God's Word (Matthew 27:25). The conflict will be fully resolved when Christ comes again, and Satan, who appears to be having his own way, will be overthrown and destroyed at Christ's coming (2 Thessalonians 2:8).

MURDER

Disobedience to God's Word and giving in to jealousy and anger led Cain to murder his brother. Five generations later Lamech, led away by physical appetite, defied God's law, and married two women. His anti-God nature led him to murder too. Centuries later, people who thought they knew better than God, cried out, 'Take him away! Crucify him' (John 19:15). We know who is at the source of murder (John 8:44) and know that God has pronounced judgment on him (Revelation 20:10). Thank God, those who put their trust in Him already enjoy the blessings of His kingdom (Colossians 1:13) and look forward to the coming reality of His glorious reign (Matthew 25:31-34).

HOPE

Adam and Eve were blessed with a replacement for Abel (Genesis 4:25). With the birth of Seth came a line of men who relied, not on themselves, but on God. They began to 'call on the name of the Lord'. This was proof of their faith in God. Later, through the same line would come the altar (Genesis 12:8) and an attitude of heart which regarded Jehovah as unutterably sacred (Exodus 20:7). The Israelites offered their sacrifices as atonement for their souls (Leviticus 17:11). Today, because of Christ, an eternal sacrifice, God's Word declares 'Everyone who calls on the name of the Lord will be saved' (Romans 10:13).

We shall later discover that Christ (the promised Seed of the woman in Genesis 3:15) came of the line of Seth.

RAMPANT GODLESSNESS – AND GOD'S MAN

DAY 1   *Genesis 6:1-2 (Job 1:6; 2:1; 38:7, see NIV footnotes).*
a) Discuss what the Scriptures imply about the sons of God (GNB 'heavenly beings').
b) What does the latter part of verse 2 indicate?

DAY 2   *Genesis 6:3-4.*
a) How long is God going to give these people to repent? And us (2 Corinthians 6:2)?
b) Read verse 4 in various translations. How did the 'giants' (LB) appear?

DAY 3   *Genesis 6:5-8.*
a) How did God feel about the state of the earth?
b) How did God purpose to deal with such blatant defiance?

DAY 4   *Genesis 6:9-13.*
a) How is Noah described here?
b) In this corrupt society how could Shem, Ham and Japheth escape contamination?

DAY 5   *Genesis 6:14-16; 2:5-6; Hebrews 11:7.*
a) How might godless men have reacted to Noah building the ark?
b) How did Noah react to them?
c) Can you visualise how big the ark was?

DAY 6   *Genesis 6:17; 2 Peter 2:5; Matthew 24:37-39.*
a) What further insight do we get into life in Noah's day?
b) What parallel does Jesus say exists between the flood and His coming again?

DAY 7   *Genesis 6:18-22.*
a) With whom did God establish His covenant?
b) What was to happen to all the creatures God had created (v.7)?
c) Name the outstanding quality of Noah's character.

RAMPANT GODLESSNESS – AND GOD'S MAN

WICKEDNESS
The 'sons of God' (AV) is a controversial and unresolved issue. Were they the descendants of Seth who 'took' (whether in rightful marriage or not) the daughters of Cain? Then we are left with the problem that their progeny were giants rather than normal human beings!

Scripture (such as the Job references in our study) refers to created beings, possibly fallen angels acting in opposition to God. Could these have been termed 'sons of God'? Satan and his angels were certainly capable of deceiving and inhabitating human as well as animal bodies (e.g. serpent) for their own evil ends. Were they responsible for pushing people further and further into lustful living? The offspring of these unions were not only monsters in size, but also in wickedness, and they seemed to lead the way in lustful and satanic activity which became universal corruption and violence. The world certainly lay in the lap of the wicked one.

> ... God regretted that He had made man.

THE GRACE OF GOD
The word 'grace' or 'favour' is used here for the first time in Scripture (Genesis 6:8). God found in Noah a man ready to respond to His will in obedient faith. In the midst of wickedness one man is uniquely righteous (vv.8-9). He was a preacher of righteousness (2 Peter 2:5). His sons described him as perfect in his generation (v.9). Noah did all that God commanded him (v.22). He walked with God (v.9). He was a man great in faith (Hebrews 11:7).

Satan sought to corrupt the whole world. But the one man he would have loved to destroy was invulnerable under the protection of the grace of God.

THE PLACE OF SALVATION
God's way of escape from judgment and destruction was the ark. And there was only one door in it. Once you were in, that was it! Judgment fell on all who were without. Noah alone qualified for entrance. He was counted righteous through the obedience of faith. He believed God and acted on His instructions. The scorn and hatred of godless men did not influence him away from God.

Our world today is not too different!

'The world will be at ease – banquets and parties and weddings – just as it was in Noah's time before the sudden coming of the flood; people wouldn't believe what was going to happen until the flood actually arrived and took them all away. So shall my coming be' (Matthew 24:37-39 LB).

'(God) isn't really slow about his promised return, even though it sometimes seems that way. But he is waiting, for the good reason that he is not willing that any should perish, and he is giving more time for sinners to repent' (2 Peter 3:9 LB).

Are you safe in the ark – Christ Jesus?

'No one who has become part of God's family makes a practice of sinning, for Christ, God's Son, holds him securely and the devil cannot get his hands on him. We know that we are children of God and that all the rest of the world around us is under Satan's power and control. And we know that Christ, God's Son, has come to help us understand and find the true God. And now we are in God because we are in Jesus Christ his Son who is the only true God; and he is eternal Life' (1 John 5:18-20 LB).

JUDGMENT BY WATER

DAY 1　　*Genesis 7:1-3.*
a) What reason does God give for welcoming Noah into the ark?
b) How was Noah to select animals for the ark?

DAY 2　　*Genesis 7:4-12; 6:16.*
a) How would the flood come about?
b) How did Noah and the animals enter the ark? What in John 10:9 does this remind us of?

DAY 3　　*Genesis 7:13-18.*
a) Who closed the door of the ark?
b) What happened as the waters rose?

DAY 4　　*Genesis 7:19-24.*
a) What happened to the earth's populace? Why?
b) How long did the flood last?

DAY 5　　*Genesis 8:1-4.*
a) How did the waters start to dry up?
b) Where did the ark come to rest?

DAY 6　　*Genesis 8:5-14.*
a) Describe how Noah assessed it was time to disembark.
b) Can you visualise how the earth would have appeared to Noah?

DAY 7　　*Genesis 8:15-22.*
a) What instructions did God give?
b) How did Noah react?
c) Was God pleased? What did He promise?

JUDGMENT BY WATER

FAITH – PATIENCE
It was nearly 100 years after God spoke to Noah that the flood came! All that time Noah warned and preached and went steadily on with the building of the ark. Finally, God said 'Go into the ark'. Interesting? God was with him! All those years God had been with him too.

DELUGE
Up till now the earth had been moistened by mist. Somehow the huge blanket of invisible water was released by the power of God and it was as if the windows of heaven opened like a sluice gate and down it came. The springs 'burst forth' too, and the ark (miracle of God's planning) remained stable and buoyant in the swirling waters. Forty days – forty nights non stop! And the Bible indicates that it was worldwide (Genesis 7:19).

SAFETY FOR THE RIGHTEOUS
It is interesting to know that:
Noah was in the ark seven days before the rain came (7:4, 10).
It began to rain on the 17th day of the second month of Noah's 600th year (7:11).
It rained 40 days (7:12).
The waters lasted 150 days (7:24; 8:3).
The ark rested on the Ararat Mountains on the 17th day of the seventh month (8:4).
The ark's covering was removed on the first day of the first month of Noah's 601st year (8:13).
The ark was vacated on the 27th day of the second month (8:14-19).
Noah and company were in the ark for one year and 17 days (5 months floating and 7 months on the mountain waiting for the waters to abate).

What an experience! What busy people Noah and his family must have been feeding and caring for such a large household!

DESTRUCTION FOR THE DISOBEDIENT
Neither man, animal or vegetation escaped the judgment by water. Man had been well warned. God had been very patient. His Word had come to pass. 'By these waters also the world of that time was deluged and destroyed' (2 Peter 3:6). God's world of life and beauty had become a desolate wilderness.

THANKSGIVING
Noah built an altar to the Lord. This is the first of many built in memorial and thanksgiving to God. His sacrifice came from the 'clean' animals and birds which had

sheltered in the ark. Can you imagine how Noah and his family would lift glad hearts (even in the midst of a desolate world) to God for His protection and provision for them? How's your spirit of praise?

PROMISE
God will never put His creation through judgment by flood again. Yet man's heart is still evil. Because man cannot help himself, he desperately needs the grace of God. God must judge sin, but 'He is patient with you, not wanting anyone to perish (2 Peter 3:9). God's curse on sin must prevail until the new earth of His promise appears (Revelation 22:3).

His offer of mercy is open to all ... Oh that men would respond and receive His grace ... the next judgment will be one of fire (2 Peter 3:7).

THE NEW WORLD

DAY 1   *Genesis 9:1-4.*
a) Do you see a repeat of Genesis 1:28 here?
b) What was added to man's diet after the flood?

DAY 2   *Genesis 9:5-7.*
a) What price did God put on a man's life?
b) Why does God keep repeating this injunction to replenish the earth?

DAY 3   *Genesis 9:8-12.*
a) With whom did God establish His covenant?
b) What was His promise?

DAY 4   *Genesis 9:13-19.*
a) What should you think of when you see a rainbow?
b) How did the earth once again become populated?

DAY 5   *Genesis 9:20-23.*
a) What occupation did Noah follow?
b) How did his sons react when they saw him drunk?
c) What does this incident have to say to us (1 Corinthians 10:12)?

DAY 6   *Genesis 9:24-25.*
a) What did Noah realise when he roused from his stupor?
b) How did he react to Ham who had discovered his condition?

DAY 7   *Genesis 9:26-29.*
a) What did Noah predict for Shem and Japheth?
b) How long did he live after the flood?

THE NEW WORLD

MAN'S RESPONSIBILITY UNDER GOD

It is interesting that, unlike Adam (Genesis 1:26) Noah was not instructed to rule the animal world. In fact, it is evident that there is now a fear of man in beasts, birds and fish, (though not in domestic animals) that did not exist before the flood.

God indicated to Noah areas of authority in the setting up of the new society. Man, made in God's image, is to be protected from murder. Capital punishment is instituted. God created life, man is not to destroy it. More laws would have to be made regarding areas which could lead to murder: robbery, adultery, etc.

There are cases in the Bible where justice is tempered with mercy when the guilty party becomes repentant, e.g., God gave David pardon (although he had committed adultery and murder) because he repented (1 Chronicles 29:28). The woman taken in adultery should have been killed by stoning but Jesus saw her repentant heart and set her free (John 8:3-11).

DIET

People were vegetarians till the time of the flood (Genesis 1:29-30) but now they are allowed to eat meat (Genesis 9:3-4). God stresses blood as the life factor and says it was not to be eaten.

GOD'S PROMISE

This was for both man and the animal world (9:15). God would never again judge the world with a universal flood. His covenant would hold good not only for Noah's generation, but for all those to come (9:12).

The rainbow would serve as a sign or reminder to both God and man that God would keep His promise. Recently I heard my little granddaughter warbling away 'I can see a rainbow'. What a lovely thought! I'm sure Noah and his family, having been through the flood, would often have had occasion to sing thankfully and confidently about the God who keeps His promises.

RACES AND NATIONS

The origin of races and nations is fascinating. It is amazing that, stemming from a common ancestor, there are now over 200 nations and over 6,000 language groups.

The whole earth became populated through the proliferation of Noah's three sons. Although still subject to satanic temptation, at this stage they were God-fearing and children of God's covenant. The incidence of Noah's moral lapse is sad and reminds us that we are to be 'self-controlled and alert. Your enemy the devils prowls around like a roaring lion looking for someone to devour' (1 Peter 5:8).

Noah resented that Ham had discovered him in his drunken state (there is some inference that Ham displayed a different attitude from his brothers' who sought to prevent their father's embarrassment), and predicted blessing and fellowship between Japheth and Shem and servitude upon Ham's descendants.

FILL THE EARTH

Noah's sons were doing a very good job! Not only were they to populate the world, but they would feel it a God-given duty to fill the earth with 'the knowledge of the LORD as the waters cover the sea' (Isaiah 11:9), and to teach men 'to call on the name of the LORD' (Genesis 4:26).

History reveals that the Japhite nations were Indo-European; the Semites were Jews, Arabs, Syrians, Persians, etc.; and the Hamites African, Mongol, Indian, and South Sea Islanders.

True to Noah's prediction, though not exclusively, the descendants of Japheth and Shem were more involved in spiritual and intellectual pursuits, while the descendants of Ham were more inclined towards trades, farming and labouring (see 9:26-27).

EMERGING NATIONS

DAY 1 *Genesis 10:1-9.*
a) Were Noah's sons obeying God's injunction in 9:1?
b) Can you put verse 5 into your own words (see the Living Bible)?
c) Who in these verses is remembered as being powerful?

DAY 2 *Genesis 10:10-20; 12:5; 18:20.*
a) What two cities were noted for their wickedness?
b) Which land became the Promised Land?

DAY 3 *Genesis 10:21-32.*
a) Does this table of nations bore or excite you?
b) Have you noticed anything special in Genesis 10:5,31?

DAY 4 *Genesis 11:1-4.*
a) Does verse1 contradict 10:5,31?
b) Does the 'people plot' of verses 3 and 4 say anything to you?

DAY 5 *Genesis 11:5-9; 1:26.*
a) How did God react to their plan?
b) What words indicate that there is more than one Person in the Godhead (Genesis 1:26)?

DAY 6 *Genesis 11:10-28.*
a) Does the list of names confuse you? Turn to Luke 3. Reading backwards from verse 38 list the family tree down to the birth of Jesus.
c) Who of importance is listed in Genesis 11:26

DAY 7 *Genesis 11:29-32.*
a) Who was Sarai?
b) Where did Abraham originally live?

EMERGING NATIONS

THE TABLE OF NATIONS

This was kept accurately by each successive generation so that a very comprehensive record can be compiled as we study God's Word. The line of succession from Adam to Jesus (the Promised Seed of the woman) is the all-important one. A study of both Japheth and Ham's line, and indeed of many of the individuals would be most enlightening. For brevity, however, the account in Luke 3 working back from verse 38, is easiest to follow.

The son of God, Adam - Seth - Enos - Kenan - Mahalaleel - Jared - Enoch -Methuselah - Lamech - Noah - Shem - Arphaxad - Cainan - Shelah - Eber - Peleg - Reu - Serug - Nahor - Terah to Abraham, the point we have just reached in Bible narrative, is twenty generations. In Luke you can trace through the next fifty generations to the coming of Jesus.

REBELLION AGAIN

As the population increased an anti-God spirit began to appear again. Ham's oldest son, resenting Noah's curse, no doubt, named his son Nimrod – 'Let us rebel'. Nimrod made his presence known. He was a hunter. He knew how to manipulate and motivate men (Genesis 10:9; 1 Chronicles 1:10). Some suggest he instigated the building of the Tower of Babel (Genesis 11:4,8,9) in defiance of God.

God brought a confusion of tongues where there had been but one common language. He scattered the nations worldwide in an effort to hinder communication and inhibit godlessness. 'Therefore is the name of it called Babel, because the Lord did there confound the language of all the earth' (Genesis 11:9).

Look at Zephaniah 3:9 in the Living Bible: 'At that time I will change the speech of my returning people to pure Hebrew so that all can worship the Lord together.'
God has promised that when the day comes that the nations all follow His will in obedience to His Word, the confusion of Babel will be reversed.

Dr. Morris comments:
'A foregleam of this miraculous elimination of the language barrier' came on the day of Pentecost. When the Holy Spirit descended, God enabled the disciples to declare the wonderful works of God in many languages so that many could understand (Acts 2:6-11).

Won't it be a marvellous day when the hearts and tongues of all God's children can praise Him as One!

PARADISE REGAINED

We began this series by looking back to the very beginning of everything, and also looking forward to the time when God will again create everything new.

Let's bring together now God's wonderful future plan for His creation.

DAY 1   *Compare Genesis 1:1 with Revelation 21:1,5 and Genesis 1:14-16 with Revelation 21:23-27.*
a) What differences can you find?
b) Are there are similarities?

DAY 2   *Compare Genesis 2:8-12 with Revelation 21:10-11,24-26.*
a) How would you describe the first man's home?
b) What can you discover about man's eternal home?

DAY 3   *Compare Genesis 2:20-24 with Revelation 19:7-9.*
a) What two marriages are described here?
b) Who is the bride in the second one (Ephesians 5:25-32)?

DAY 4   *Compare Genesis 3:1 with Revelation 20:7-10.*
a) Where did the devil first appear to man?
b) What is his ultimate destination?
c) What can you discover about hell in 2 Thessalonians 1:6-9?

DAY 5   *Compare Genesis 3:14-19 with Revelation 21:4,27; 22:3.*
a) What kind of suffering came as a result of sin?
b) What things will have no place in the heavenly city?

DAY 6   *Compare Genesis 3:23-24 with Revelation 22:1-4,14.*
a) What is mentioned in both these references?
b) How is it described in Revelation?
c) Why is man to be in the city when he was sent out of the garden?

DAY 7   *Read Revelation 22:12-21 thoughtfully.*
Pick out one thing that particularly impresses you. Share this with the group.

PARADISE REGAINED

The beginning was great! We messed things up! But there is a glorious future ahead!

Don't you think our studies have made it clear that we are travellers bound for heaven? Anyone going on a journey must make sure that his travel papers are in order, and entrance to overseas countries secured. Heaven is no exception. Here is some vital information:

Accommodation: Top grade only. 'In my Father's house are many rooms ... I am going there to prepare a place for you' (John 14:2).

Passports: Absolutely essential. 'Nothing impure will ever enter it, nor will anyone who does what is shameful or deceitful, but only those whose names are written in the Lamb's Book of Life' (Revelation 21:27).

Departure time: This is not announced. Be prepared to leave at short notice. 'It is not for you to know the times or dates the Father has set by his own authority' (Acts 1:7).

Tickets: You have a written pledge that guarantees your journey, but you must claim it, and keep its promises. 'Whoever hears my word, and believes him who sent me has eternal life ... he has crossed over from death to life' (John 5:24).

Customs: Only one declaration necessary: 'Confess ... believe ... be saved' (Romans 10:9).

Immigration: All travellers are classified as immigrants, as they are taking up permanent residence in a NEW COUNTRY. The quota is open. 'They were longing for a better country, a heavenly one ... God ... has prepared a city for them' (Hebrews 11:16).

Luggage: None can be taken. Everything you need is there. 'We brought nothing into the world, and we can take nothing out of it' (1 Timothy 6:7).

Air Travel: Those going directly by air must watch for indications of imminent departure. 'The Lord himself will come ... we who are still alive ... will be caught up ... to meet the Lord in the air' (1 Thessalonians 4:16-17).

Medical Precautions: No injections needed, as disease and sickness never occur. 'There will be no more death or mourning or crying or pain' (Revelation 21:4).

Currency: Send ahead – as large deposits as possible. 'Store up for yourselves treasure in heaven' (Matthew 6:20).

ANSWER GUIDE

The following pages contain an Answer Guide. It is recommended that answers to the questions be attempted before turning to this guide. It is only a guide and the answers given should not be treated as exhaustive.

THE BEGINNING OF EVERYTHING

You will have to approach this study very prayerfully, and be quite firm about the group keeping strictly to discussion 'on the point'. Controversy over evolution, critical comments on authorship, etc., will prove time-wasting, as even scholars who have made life-studies on these issues are not agreed on such points.

Urge the group to come to God's Word with an open mind, a receptive and prayerful spirit. As in all our studies, we want people to be tuned in to what God is saying to them personally, so that the practical truths discovered will help them in everyday living and further confirm their faith in a personal God and Saviour.

Note from Scripture that Moses was instructed to write down the words he heard from God (Exodus 34:27). The Pentateuch, that is the first five books of the Bible, is referred to as 'the Law of Moses' (Daniel 9:11) and the 'Book of Moses' (2 Chronicles 35:12). When the New Testament quotes from any one of these books it states 'Moses said ...' (Mark 7:10).

Genesis is basic to all the other sixty five books of the Bible. Anyone who earnestly desires to understand the whole of Scripture needs a good understanding of what Genesis says. In this series of studies we will cover only the first eleven chapters as outlined in our introductory study. Subsequently the studies on the lives of Abraham, Jacob and Joseph can be used to fully cover the whole of Genesis.

It would be good to major on the statement, 'In the beginning God created the heavens and the earth' in the first session together. This is the Biblical declaration of the origin of this material universe. God spoke and worlds were framed! God called all things into being by the word of His power. Interpretations of the method God used may vary, but the truth of the fact remains. See Hebrews 11:3. Read this verse in several translations.

DAY 1   a) God was always there.
b) God.
b) God moved by His Spirit and out of a 'formless and empty' earth created day and night.

DAY 2   a) God made the sky, spread overhead, like a canopy.
b) This divided the upper waters (cloud) from the lower water.

DAY 3   a) Now God created and named the land and sea.
b) The vegetable kingdom appeared: grass, herbs, trees; all capable of reproducing themselves.

DAY 4   a) The sun, moon and stars are now created.
b) God simply spoke and it all happened!

DAY 5   a) God stocked the oceans with fish and sea animals and the air with birds.
b) They all had powers of procreation.

DAY 6   a) The animal kingdom.
b) In this crowning act of creation God made man in His own image and with authority over every other creature.

DAY 7   a) Creation is a result of God's plan and work; it is now complete.
b) These verses underline that God created everything.

DAY 1   a) The LORD God.
             b) Genesis 1:9-10.

DAY 2   a) Man was formed from the dust of the ground.
             b) God breathed His life into the clay figure.
             c) No; animal and marine life were directly created.

DAY 3   a) In the east, in Eden.
             b) Beautiful and useful!
             c) The tree of life and the tree of the knowledge of good and evil.

DAY 4   a) Care for the garden and guard its sanctity (it was God's place!).
             b) He was forbidden to eat from this tree. Careful obedience of this command would demonstrate his devotion to God.

DAY 5   a) God said he would die.
             b) Blessing comes through being aware of, meditating upon and carefully obeying God's word. The tragic alternative brought about by disobedience should also motivate us to obey.

DAY 6   a) He saw it was 'good'.
             b) God saw it was not good for man not to have a human companion. God was going to make a 'helper' for him.

DAY 7   a) No. Man didn't find his partner in the animal world.
             b) God took a rib from the man's body and formed a woman from it.
             c) It was His means for the propagation of the human race. God intended children to be born from this union.
             Marriage is to provide companionship for life, while the child-parent relationship is temporary.

DAY 1   a) God is a loving, caring creator who has provided abundantly for His creatures – in a perfect paradise.

b) The serpent. Adam and Eve are banished from the Garden of Eden.

DAY 2   a) Great dragon, devil, Satan.

b) 'Prince of this world', 'god of this age', 'ruler of the kingdom of this age.'

DAY 3   He was a created angel full of beauty, perhaps the chiefest, highest angel (v.14). Created perfect and remained so until the sin of pride was found in him (v.17).

DAY 4   a) Answers will depend on translation used. NIV has 'morning star' and son of the dawn'.

b) It focuses more on Satan's pride (referred to in Ezekiel 28): his desire was to be equal with God.

DAY 5   They assist and defend God's people; they worship God; they perform specific functions for God.

DAY 6   a) He steals God's word; he is cunning, a liar and a murderer.

b) The complete opposite.

DAY 7   a) It was good, indeed 'very good' (Genesis 1:31).

b) Satan used the serpent as his mouthpiece.

DAY 1   a) He cast doubt on God's word; he tried to confuse her.
She added to what God had said by introducing the prohibition 'must not touch it'.
b) Many dangers. We lose sight of what He has said; the reference in Revelation highlights that those who tamper with it will not inherit eternal life.

DAY 2   a) He blatantly contradicts God's word; he casts doubt on God's goodness, he majors on the prohibition by implying that it is restrictive in their development of becoming equal with God (v.5).
b) Yes, she obeyed the devil and disobeyed God. Adam likewise disobeyed and through his disobedience sin entered the world.

DAY 3   a) Physical (good for food).
Emotional (lovely to look at).
Mental (desirable for wisdom).
b) By refusing any dialogue with the devil; by maintaining faith in God's word. We need to be constantly wearing God's armour.

DAY 4   a) Their eyes were opened; they now knew evil as a real force within them.
b) Shame, remorse and fear. They were ashamed of their nakedness (innocence gone); they tried to 'cover up' their sin and hide from God; they were afraid of Him. Their spirits had died.

DAY 5   a) Instead of confessing their sin, they blamed others.
b) Eve would suffer in childbirth; nature would be affected; decay would set in; loss of eternal life.

DAY 6   a) Three: between the serpent and the woman; between the descendants of the woman and the serpent (implying conflict between believers and non-believers, John 8:44); between one descendant of the woman and the serpent.
b) This is a promise of a coming Redeemer, later identified as the Lord Jesus, who would achieve victory through His death and resurrection.

DAY 7   a) He shed the blood of an animal and provided a skin for a covering.
b) Someone had to die for our sins: this was the Lord Jesus whose blood was shed for us.

DAY 1   a) Cain was a farmer – Abel a shepherd.
              b) Abel offered his sacrifice in faith ; he came to God in the right way (they probably both were aware of the importance of a blood offering, but only Abel approached God in this way).

DAY 2   a) They led him to murder his brother. (How the devil gets in!)
              b) He would no longer be successful as a farmer; he became a nomad.

DAY 3   a) No. God promised to protect Cain from death at the hand of an avenger.
              b) Cain moved away to the east of Eden (out of close touch with God?), married, had a son, started to build a city and introduced industry.

DAY 4   a) The sixth.
              b) Lamech, Cain's great-great-great grandson.

DAY 5   a) Some people began to 'call' or use the Lord's name in worship.
              b) That man had been made in the 'likeness of God'.

DAY 6   a) Adam died (physically) at the ripe old age of 930 years!
              b) It is amazing how God preserved, through His chosen channels, these details of the beginning of the human race – from thousands of years before Christ came.

DAY 7   a) Enoch 'walked with God' and went to be with God without physically dying!
              b) 969 years.
              b) Methuselah's grandson was named Noah. His name is associated with 'comfort'. He had three sons named Shem, Ham and Japheth.

DAY 1
a) The implication is they were angelic rather than human beings.
b) These were self-pleasing and lustful relationships.

DAY 2
a) Their life span would be 120 years or, they would have 120 years before judgment came.
We don't know how long we've got.
b) Probably from the alliance of angelic beings with human beings.

DAY 3
a) He saw wickedness rampant, man obsessed with evil. He was grieved that He had made man.
b) All the ungodly would be destroyed. Righteous Noah would live.

DAY 4
a) He was just, perfect and walked with God.
b) Most likely through godly parental example and influence (and hard work!).

DAY 5
a) There was no sign of rain or water so they probably thought him mad.
b) Their scorn didn't touch him – he went right on with God's work.
c) About 140 metres long, 23 metres wide, 13.5 metres high, big enough to carry 125,000 sheep and fodder!

DAY 6
a) It was godless; people were engrossed in their everyday life unconcerned about the coming judgment
b) Like the flood, Jesus' return would be sudden and unexpected; people would not be ready for it. They will not be able to avoid its consequences.

DAY 7
a) Noah.
b) All would be destroyed, except those kept to preserve the species.
c) Obedience to God.

DAY 1   a) He was the only righteous man to be found.
b) A pair from each class was to be selected to preserve the species. Seven pairs of each 'clean' animal were to be included.

DAY 2   a) It would rain and rain (for the first time!) and subterranean springs gush forth.
b) By the only door in the ark.
It reminds us that Jesus is our only way of salvation.

DAY 3   a) God shut Noah in (because he was right with God).
b) The ark floated safely on top of the waters.

DAY 4   a) Everyone was utterly destroyed. They had obviously refused to heed Noah's warning and now God had shut them out.
b) 150 days.

DAY 5   a) The rain stopped and a wind sprang up.
b) The ark rested on the mountain of Ararat (south west of the Black Sea and near to the Eden location mentioned in Study 2, Day 3).

DAY 6   a) Noah released a raven which kept circling over the water. Then he released a dove which returned, not having found a resting place. At intervals of seven days he sent the dove out again. The first time it returned with an olive leaf, the second time it didn't return. The water had abated.
b) The earth must have been a slimy, desolate waste.

DAY 7   a) To come out of the ark with all his family, animals, birds and creatures.
b) Noah built an altar and made a sacrifice of thanksgiving to God.
c) The Lord was pleased with his sacrifice and promised never again to curse the ground or destroy life in this way.

DAY 1   a) Yes; Noah was given the same instructions as Adam: replenish and fill the earth.
          b) Meat was introduced as a food.

DAY 2   a) Man must not destroy man who had been made in God's image. The penalty for murder was death.
          b) Probably to encourage man to rise to his God-given responsibility.

DAY 3   a) Noah, his sons, their offspring and every living creature.
          b) He would never again destroy the earth and its life by flood.

DAY 4   a) We should praise God that He has kept that promise made to Noah!
          b) Through the progeny of Noah's sons.

DAY 5   a) He became a vineyard keeper.
          b) Shem and Japheth covered his nakedness. (Remember Genesis 3:21?)
          c) 1 Corinthians 10:12 warns us to be aware that we can fall into sin if we don't keep relying on God.

DAY 6   a) His drunkenness had been discovered and someone had covered him.
          b) He pronounced a curse of servitude on Ham's line.

DAY 7   a) Blessing and enlargement; Shem would dwell in the tents of Japheth. Canaan (Ham's son) would serve them both.
          c) 350 years.

DAY 1   a) Yes; the population was increasing fast!
b) The Living Bible paraphrases it neatly.
c) Nimrod – believed to be the instigator of the Tower of Babel.

DAY 2   a) Sodom and Gomorrah mentioned in Genesis 18:20. See also 2 Peter 2:6.
b) Canaan – destined to be the land of promise for Israel.

DAY 3   a) If we follow through these names carefully we see how the life of the Promised Seed (Genesis 3:15) is being preserved.
b) People were speaking in different languages.

DAY 4   a) Chronologically the verses in chapter 10 follow chapter 11:4.
b) The people are again beginning to manifest an anti-God spirit.

DAY 5   a) He gave them different languages and forced them to move away from each other.
b) The words of God, 'let us'. This foreshadows the doctrine of the Trinity which is unfolded in its fullness in the New Testament.

DAY 6   a) The Luke genealogy is simpler to follow! Luke gives us 76 generations from Adam to Jesus which covers 4000 years.
b) 'Abram' better known as Abraham.

DAY 7   a) Sarai was Abraham's wife.
b) In a city called 'Ur of the Chaldeans'.

DAY 1   a) Differences: no sea, no sun, no moon, no night, everything new, city illuminated by the glory of God, free access to the city.
b) Similarities: God created both so that He might have fellowship with man and man with Him.

DAY 2   a) It was a luxurious and fruitful garden with an abundance of gold nearby.
b) A city, ablaze with the glory of God and open to all the nations.

DAY 3   a) The marriage of Adam and Eve, and that of the Lamb of God.
b) The church – the Bride of Christ.

DAY 4   a) In the beautiful garden of Eden!
b) The lake of fire.
c) A place completely cut off from the presence of the Lord.

DAY 5   a) The serpent is cursed, women will suffer in childbirth, man will toil and struggle for an existence.
b) No more curse or suffering – no tears, sorrow or pain.

DAY 6   a) The tree of Life:
b) It bears fruit every month and its leaves are for the healing the nations.
c) Man was banished because of sin but has entrance to the eternal city through faith in Christ's atoning work.

DAY 7   a) God is a just God and has decreed the only way into His eternal presence. His generous invitation is extended to all: 'Come'.

THE WORD WORLDWIDE

We first heard of WORD WORLDWIDE over 20 years ago when Marie Dinnen, its founder, shared excitedly about the wonderful way ministry to a needy woman had exploded to touch many lives. It was great to see the Word of God being made central in the lives of thousands of men and women, then the life changing effects that resulted when they applied the Word into their circumstances. Over the years the vision for WORD WORLDWIDE has not dimmed in the hearts of those who are involved in this ministry. God is still at work through His Word and in today's self-seeking society, the Word is even more relevant to those who desire true meaning and purpose in life. WORD WORLDWIDE is a ministry of WEC International, an interdenominational missionary society, whose sole purpose for existence is to see Christ known, loved and worshipped by all, particularly those who have yet to hear of His wonderful name. This ministry is a vital part of our work and we warmly recommend the WORD WORLDWIDE 'Geared for Growth' Bible studies to you. We know that as you study His Word you will be enriched in your personal walk with Christ. It is our hope that as you are blessed through these studies, you will find opportunities to help others find a personal relationship with Jesus. As a mission we would encourage you to work with us to make Christ known to the ends of the earth.

Stewart & Jean Moulds – British Directors, WEC International.

A full list of over 50 'Geared for Growth' studies can be obtained from:

ENGLAND   John & Ann Edwards
5 Louvain Terrace, Hetton-le Hole, Tyne & Wear, DH5 9PP
Tel. 0191 5262803   Email: rhysjohn.edwards@virgin.net

IRELAND   Steffney Preston
33 Harcourts Hill, Portadown, Craigavon, N. Ireland, BT62 3RE
Tel. 028 3833 7844   Email: sa.preston@talk21.com

SCOTLAND   Margaret Halliday
10 Douglas Drive, Newton Mearns, Glasgow, G77 6HR
Tel. 0141 639 8695   Email: m_halliday@excite.co.uk

WALES   William & Eirian Edwards
Penlan Uchaf, Carmarthen Road, Kidwelly, Carms., SA17 5AF
Tel. 01554 890423   Email: Penlan.uchaf@farming.co.uk

UK CO-ORDINATOR
Anne Jenkins, 2 Windermere Road, Carnforth, Lancs., LA5 9AR
Tel. 01524 734797   Email: anne@jenkins.abelgratis.com

www.wordworldwide.org.uk